THE ADVENTURES OF CARMEL DELIGHT

Featuring
Mr. Huggstable,
Mr. Blu Collar And
Mr. Vandalicious

The Adventures of Carmel Delight, Featuring Mr. Huggstable, Mr. Blu Collar and Mr. Vandalicious

Published in the United States, Intuitive Thoughts Publishing Company

Email: Spignotta59@Yahoo.com

First Edition

ISBN: 979-8-9872934-1-6

THE ADVENTURES OF CARMEL DELIGHT

Featuring
Mr. Huggstable,
Mr. Blu Collar And
Mr. Vandalicious

Spignotta Milam

Table of Contents

Section One: Mr. Computer Love 1

- There He Goes 4
- He Calls Me Darlin' 5
- You on Some Grown Man Shit 6
- Having Moments 8
- Vulnerability 9
- Silent Observation 10
- Just You 11
- Quiet Storm 12
- Affirmations of You 13
- Dearest One 14
- Mr. Intrigue 15
- You, You 16
- Going Ghost 17
- Addictive Vibes of Discontent 19
- Good Morning 20
- Adolescent Shenanigans 21
- Love at First Sight 23
- Sayonara 27
- Darlin' No More 29
- Missing the Idealistic Presence of You 30
- Mirage of Myself 32

Section Two: Dallas Rising 33

- Venus & Mars 35
- Purple Passion 37
- The Voice 38

- Pity the Brother 39
- Dilemma 41
- Agony and Ecstasy 43
- Alpha Omega, Omega Alpha 45
- My Heart Is Black 47
- AutoCadding 48
- I Can Hear You Smiling 49
- I Can Make It Rain 50
- Intensive Thought 51
- Sexy Vocal Cords 52
- She Butter 53
- Intimate Sessions 54
- Just Being Nasty 55
- Logitech 56
- I Hear You 57
- Miles Apart 58
- Mr. No, No, No, No, No 60
- Robber Baron 61
- Sweet Serenity 62
- Take a Minute 63
- Tasty Love 64
- The Joneses 65
- Thoughts of You 66
- Today 67
- Whipping Stick Love 68
- Wounded Warrior 69
- You Are Genuine 70
- Memories 71
- Since You Died 73
- Grief Consumes Me 76

Section Three: Raw Sensuality.................................. 79

- ❖ Single Ain't Shit..........80
- ❖ I Want a Man..........81
- ❖ I Need a Man That Can Put It Down..........82
- ❖ I Want a Man I Can Take Outside..........83
- ❖ What I Want from You..........84
- ❖ Lying Eyes..........85
- ❖ One to Put It Down and One to Be Around..........86
- ❖ Wolf in Sheep's Clothing..........87
- ❖ Ben—Done..........89
- ❖ If I Could Slow You Down, I'd Show You Something..........91
- ❖ Is It Spring or Are You Cold?..........92
- ❖ I'm a Nurturer, Not a Nurse..........93
- ❖ I Can't Lay Down with My Checking Account..........95
- ❖ Dingwat..........96
- ❖ Depression..........97
- ❖ You're a Snake in the Ass..........98
- ❖ Fleabag Reality Check..........100
- ❖ Stop It!..........102
- ❖ Fury of a Woman's Scorn..........104
- ❖ Ball, Book or Bike..........106
- ❖ Young Blood..........108
- ❖ Vandalicious..........110
- ❖ Brudda..........112
- ❖ Around Midnight..........113
- ❖ At the Crack of Dawn..........114
- ❖ Leroy's Kind of Love..........115
- ❖ Mr. Blu Collar Man..........117
- ❖ Mr. Huggstable..........119

❖ You Know How to Love Me 120
❖ Rain 121
❖ Rubber-Broke Babies 122
❖ Wounded 124
❖ Time Shuttle 125
❖ There You Were 126
❖ You and I 128
❖ The Future Is Ours 129

ABOUT THE AUTHOR 130

Section One

Mr. Computer Love

We went from the perfect blending of two intelligent minds who were spontaneous comforts to each other to fizzled ships heading in opposite directions.

All of my computers were in distress. I couldn't access my laptop because I had forgotten my password, my desktop would not allow me to access the microphone to hear anything when I was on Zoom calls, and I had just gotten a job that required me to do Zoom calls and tele-mental health on the computer, but I had no equipment that was adequate to do that.

I happened to be discussing my frustrations with my hairdresser, and she told me she had the perfect person who could handle it all, and that is how we met.

From the moment I met him, I felt very comfortable and actually at peace around him. His offbeat humor and hearty laugh put me instantly at ease. His phenomenal skills at answering both of my computer needs within a space of 20 minutes elevated him in my eyes to computer genius.

His offer to upgrade my desktop and to bring it into the current century for no charge during a time of financial depletion made me interested in him more than ever.

It was such a refreshing, perfect beginning that he became my muse for all of the emotional feelings that had laid dormant for so long in my heart. I decided I was going to catalog these feelings through poetry, so that no matter the outcome, I was going to make money off of him.

Because I had had so many relationships that started off perfect and then disintegrated as time went on as we really got to know each other. Because we had such a rich, stable beginning, I initially ignored the warning signs.

But as they became more apparent, I included them in my poetic ramblings, which I shared with him. Until I noticed he liked to vex me just to see how my creative juices would respond, not realizing how deeply I had fallen for him. The first poem that I wrote about him, describing how I really felt, was "He Calls Me Darlin'." When I realized that there was a level of sensitivity I needed to be displayed by him that he was incapable of giving me, I wrote my version of a Dear John letter, called "Sayonara." The other poems within our "journey" that follow "Sayonara" dealt with me facing head-on my emotions and feelings regarding love, loss and *where do I go from here?* And most importantly, *what did I learn from the experience?*

He was looking for a friendship; I was looking for a relationship. It had been so long since I had been in a relationship, I had no interest or patience in going at a snail's pace, which is what he explained he wanted in the beginning. I have to take responsibility for the fact that he kept telling me he wanted to be just friends. He did dig deeper to find out what I wanted. My answer? *A complete relationship (not just sex and not dealing with a dumb ass).*

He wasn't trying to get me in bed for nearly six months. I can't say he was really, really leading me on; I was just gone. But I think he enjoyed the attention—he'd never had anybody make love to him through poetry or be that transparent in a relationship before. I think I represented meeting a tornado; even though you know it's out to destroy you, it's such a new experience, and you like it because it's new.

I think he got addicted to the uncertainty. And in the meantime, I was falling in love. During that time, he became interested in someone else and didn't feel the need to tell me. But when he stood me up on my birthday and fixed it up so that I couldn't go to where I planned to go because he waited until the last minute… I stopped.

He had already broken promises, so after my birthday, I just said no, I can't deal with this, and that was it.

There He Goes

There he goes, an astute black man quietly walking in his purpose.

Helping all he can along the way.

While waiting patiently for God's deliverance. There he goes, drawing strength every morning.

Rising up at dawn, awaiting the blue sky, which brings him joy of God's hope, renewed blessings and reminders of all the personal miracles already that have been fulfilled.

There he goes, knowing, believing with every ounce of faith that his angels have already been dispatched, and help is on the way.

He Calls Me Darlin'

When he laughs, I can feel the intensity of his chest and stomach muscles heaving as his whole body participates in the experience.

When he smiles, his eyes are like shooting stars and his cheeks radiate and expand.

When he talks in a low soothing tone, my world stops and no one exists but him.

I remain calm and appear to be relaxed, but I am feeling the intensity of his essence flow through all my intimate spaces. Yet we have only had an intimate conversation.

He is Making Love to my mind as he accepts me just the way I am. No need to be a mind reader or chameleon. Just be me.

And the Icing on the Cake is…

HE CALLS ME DARLIN'.

You on Some Grown Man Shit

Thank you GOD for searching the universe and directing my King to me. I had grown weary of dealing with boys dressed in men's clothing, camouflaging their insecurities and immaturity with exterior armors and material trappings. Their whole purpose was to seduce women into thinking Mr. Manhood has arrived. Only to discover after close examination, you too were a mama's boy; I had been duped again.

Now I have a man who is not intimidated by my strength. Nor is he put off by my brutal honesty. He welcomes a true partner who wants to lighten his load and complement his strength. He sees I give unapologetically, and he strives to reciprocate. He honors me with his smile and with gestures of being a well-raised gentleman. He opens doors and says, "Honey, call me when you get home." He sends me warm, tender wake-up affirmations of "Good Morning, Darlin'," and intimate words of peace and tranquility texts as I drift off to sleep.

He wants to be the first thought I have in the morning and the last thought I have at night. During the in-between, we accomplish our grown people task of working and serving others. This is directed by the purpose GOD has assigned to us, yet remembering to nurture and feed into our relationship.

Thank you GOD for bringing a true partner and man into my life that is operating as a helpmate. A man I want to keep.

A Man on Some Grown Man Shit.

Having Moments

I am having moments when thoughts of your gentle strength consume me.

I am having moments when I must pinch myself to see if I am dreaming. I am having moments when I want to have a distinctive praise party to thank God for bringing your kind of nurturance into my life.

I am praising GOD for as much time as he allows us to spend together. I look forward to our quality time. I am having a ball soaking into your mind, wandering through all the corridors, picking up the shattered pieces and reflecting on how you still made it out whole.

Yes, I am having moments when your gentle strength, hearty laugh, broad smile and giving heart not only consume me, but overwhelm me. How through you, my empty places are being filled.

Thank you for allowing GOD to use you to bless me and bring a level of Peace and Stability to my existence.

In the awesome name of Jesus, AMEN.

Vulnerability

Vulnerability, exposing the broken pieces for us to see. Refusing to focus on others' clapback, but instead focus on moving forward with honesty and openness.

Knowing by placing all the pieces on the table, we can work together to make the puzzle whole once more.

Vulnerability, the gift that opens doors, hearts and minds through commitment of sharing, *What the fuck is really going on?*

So, we can start at the root and grow into a better version of ourselves.

Vulnerability is my testament and word for today.

Silent Observation

As I sit here in this intellectual space, I marvel at your patience.

I marvel at your brain being full of so much useful and unuseful information. Yet, you have no desire to be a dispensary to the world.

You have a degree in silence. You have a degree in technical observation and memory recall. You are a sensitive man who uses his silence and physical demeanor to assist you in fading into the background. This is where you watch real decisions being made.

You are a thoughtful man with thoughtful perspectives regarding the underserved population. You are a shrewd-minded individual attracted to spontaneous people. You are as chiseled and orderly as a box of envelopes…

When Janet Jackson sang "Control," you were in her mind's vision.

Just You

You, a man whose presence is exhilarating.

YOU, A MAN WHOSE PASSION IS EVER PRESENT.

You, a man who has captured my heart, a man I daily try to understand.

You, a man who definitely has my attention at this moment.

You, a man whose gentleness pulls me toward him like a magnetic force field.

You, man, have you any idea how much I appreciate you for being who you are?

No imitation.

No pseudo version of someone else.

Quiet Storm

Can't wait to hear your voice as it quiets the storms within me.

Can't wait for your arms to engulf me with your warmth and soothe the savage beast within me that wants to devour your calm spirit, as a tool to help increase my patience and activate my passion to be in one accord with you. I desire to be in one accord with you spiritually, emotionally and, hopefully before I die, intimately.

I'm feeling deep care and concern for you, my King.

Affirmations of You

You know how to calm my fears. You know how to make me smile.

You know how to ignite me just by your awesome presence.

When you hold me in your arms, I smell the essence of you; it overpowers my senses.

It makes me want to melt into your strong physique and only think of you and I.

When I have a problem in your lane of expertise, I love the way you rescue me.

I love the way you use your techno-savvy persona to turn my crisis into a minute glitch in my hard drive with the swiftness of your response. You know how to vex me by not responding to my texts or calls. However, you are beginning to understand how much it hurts me to be ignored.

You are not perfect. But I still enjoy our time together. I wish we had time to explore other facets of our personalities.

There is so much more of me you have no clue about. I'm sure the same can be said about you. Hopefully we can meet on common ground and begin to explore new horizons, and not just when we are apart.

The last four months of our relationship have truly been an eye-opening experience.

Thankfully, we are still learning and growing together.

Dearest One

When I think of you, my heart smiles.

Smiles about the gentleness of your touch. Smiles about how excited I get feeling the softness of your skin. Smiles when I can close my eyes and visualize the low, soothing vocalizations I experience with every word you utter.

Smiles when I see you walk toward me and take me in your arms and squeeze me so tight I actually feel like a part of you. So much so, I sigh in disappointment when you release me to leave you and go about my life without your physical presence being there.

Loving you has been a journey… Creating positives that were there in past relationships, which had been forgotten.

Now I'm practicing patience in this journey with you in this present space and time. Watching you evolve around me, waiting for you to make the next move. Wishing and hoping I had the strength and determination to allow you to lead and not let my personal needs deter me from experiencing the relationship of a lifetime.

With you, my imagination is in overdrive.

The pleasure of your company is mine. The pleasure of uniting with your brain waves is mine. The pleasure of hearing your laughter is mine.

As I try to hold on just a little bit longer, until you are mine.

Mr. Intrigue

Thank you for being a new force of loving energy in my life. Thank you for the small ways you are consistent, like always calling me and addressing me in terms of endearment.

And laughing when my comments puzzle you and checking me when my analysis about us has gone to the left... When I am stressed out or my nerves are frazzled, I ask GOD to comfort me. When I am distressed, I will myself to remember the calming timbres of your vocal cords that create a harmonious atmosphere and eliminate my tense moments. When I am around you, time stands still until you remind me you have me scheduled in and my time with you is up. I spend time after you have left me thinking of all the other things I should have said, but you left too soon. When I am with you, your presence makes me content. My desire is to be one with you on so many levels. I love watching your facial expressions show how deep in thought you are.

Mr. Intrigue, I love you.

You, You

You, you, the arrogant self-absorbed man whom I adore.

You, you, words I say when thinking of you and wanting to insert more colorful words to emphasize my frustrations. Frustrations of being once again sucker punched by believing you would actually make time for us.

You, you, you, this man I want to know more about, yet for some reason you want me to know less…

"You, you, you" is equivalent to a parent shouting out your full name to emphasize the degree of deep trouble you are in before you race to be in front of them.

You, you, you, the more I think of you, the more my anger subsides. Because to think of life without you is not an option I am ready to accept.

You, you, you, I must acknowledge more and more your declarations of what you will do and when we will do it are becoming a montage of lies and creating a declaration of deceit.

Something I never thought would be a building block of our relationship.

Going Ghost

My perception of you was that you were a gentle, manly man.

Visions of your hardy smile and soothing voice are a reminder of your humanity.

However, I never understood your need for periodic withdrawals from me.

These retreats did not align with the strong powerful man I envisioned you to be.

Instead, it reflects a man who retreats instead of confronting something he needs to address. You once told me not to retreat. You said be authentic in all things no matter how many times it hurts. My feelings scared me by your absence, thinking something was wrong with you. I never gave up on us or you.

I remember you stating to me the day we first met that we would be friends for life. That touched me greatly and I believed you. However, you have constantly given me mixed messages throughout our six-month tenure of this relationship.

I told you I needed more of your time; you respond with less. I have become more transparent; you have become more elusive. I did not read your text or know you were on your way until I checked my phone to see who called. That was after I came back home. Considering you have subjected me to waiting in front of your apartment for hours and being a no-show on more than one occasion, I do not understand you now. You promised to take me to the movies; it has not happened. You must hate holidays. I love fellowshipping with people I care about. You have begun to reject my calls and stopped responding to my texts. You can be cruel and inhumane and very self-serving. I know you have been hurt greatly in past relationships. So have I. But I never thought you would unconsciously or consciously hurt me as a way to get back at past hurt.

I have only tried to be a best friend and encourage you. I will not apologize when I do not know what I did wrong. You owe me at least a conversation on what is going on.

Addictive Vibes of Discontent

The more layers you expose of the essence, the more I desire to know. The nuances of deep-seated family matters that tore away at deep love canals now separated and fractured, currently held together only by a pleasant memory of the past, which was so long ago it appears as a mirage.

Time, provider duties, pandemic, poverty, conflict, desire for peace to reign, all contribute to the divide widening instead of mending.

Competition, anger, disrespect, all contribute to the blind side of the real issue at hand. Generational curses keep bleeding through afflicting insecurities, doubt and trusting others being problematic.

Compromise, accepting responsibility and seeking new options of change is the only way true healing will come.

But first, everyone must share in the blame.

Good Morning

Good morning, Mr. Practicality. Good morning to the man I wish I had played the Ms. Hard to Get card with instead of being so fucking transparent.

Good morning to the man who occupies too much of my mental space during waking hours. I thank GOD you are not tormenting me in my sleep. It is the one dimension that visions of you and thoughts of you are not a focal point of my existence.

Good morning to a new day and a new way of thinking about you.

Good morning to a new perspective. Good morning to seeing more of your vulnerability and less of your perfectionism.

Good morning to a breakthrough of beginning to see you as a man who took the pathway of least resistance.

Good morning to a man to whom assumptions do not apply.

Good morning to you, a man that is as mystical as Merlin.

A man who has taken up too much of my head and heart space.

A man whom I adore.

Adolescent Shenanigans

There you go making me love you more than ever by staying up way past your bedtime to address an elephant in our relationship. There you go telling me to not give up on my love for you even if it takes a lifetime for you to get about us as I am about you, emotionally. There you are giving me a new excuse for your continuous procrastination. Especially when the things I want from you, by stating and addressing my wants, interfere with you operating in your purpose. There you go never admitting you have shortcomings. It is always the other person being self-consumed.

Even when what I want is a need to help me operate in my purpose with less stress and assist me in going from organized chaos to minimalistic order. There we were hashing out our perspectives. Like adolescent puppy love oblivious to tomorrow's work agendas. Oblivious of our age and limited rejuvenation powers that we once had long time ago in our youth. There we went operating like last night's conversation would be our last. Neither one of us wanting to stop communicating with each other. There I was opening up like a flower in the springtime that has been refreshed by a cool rain shower. Telling you too much of my personal financial business like you are a banker approving me for a loan.

Yet with the dawning of a new day, I love you more instead of less. Now you know if my finances will complement us as a union or complicate it. I know nothing about if being with you would elevate my financial security. I can only guess.

I still will never understand why a man who needs his eyes to do his job will not take the time to improve his vision, especially knowing eye disease is in his gene pool.

Here I am not ready to become more distant from you due to a new God-directed trajectory that propels me to have very little time to be with you.

There you are expecting me, Ms. Impatient Assertive, to wait forever for you to decide if being with me is the missing puzzle piece that will put up with all your bullshit.

There I am willing to try a little longer to hold out but tired of once again being duped by bullshit that what I have offered, and already given, continues to never be good enough for you to make me a priority.

Love at First Sight

Webster's Dictionary's definition of **Friend** is "showing kindly interest and goodwill, not hostility, toward an individual."

When I finally took a day to eliminate the noise of others and listen to the past statements you have made to let me know where I stand or do not stand with you, I began to realize where I misinterpreted things you stated to me. Like the first day we met, you said we would be friends for life. You also said we will communicate with each other daily. You came into my life as a digital savior. You saved my side jobs from failing and assisted me in becoming more techno savvy for the jobs God has ordained me to do. You also shared your heartache and past relationship trauma that has and will continue to impact how you will approach relationships in the future.

The parallels of our heartaches was an undoing for me. It caused such an emotional connection that I let all my guards down—something I have never done so quickly in an encounter in my life.

Your genuineness and gentleness with my assertive/ aggressiveness was a heat balm to my past hurts. Being an ultimate giver, and being removed from my major mode of giving professionally due to State of Texas limitations, exacerbated the situation. Knowing your unemployment circumstances made me want to help you anyway I could. That was what started the Sunday Dinner series. My nurturing self wanted to be your ultimate helper. Not only did I provide the meals due to you not having a car, I picked you up for them and brought you back home.

It never crossed my mind to ask for gas money. Because in my mind you were a proud man of honor who was one step away from being destitute. Your spirit of ingenuity and finding new ways to operate in your purpose made you become valiant and lovable to me. In my mind, not having a car in Texas is almost equivalent to being homeless to me. You became a new addition to my prayer list due to you seeking full-time employment, which may be limited where you could work due to transportation challenges.

Your dream of wanting to go back to school and finish your degree was also something I admired about you.

Being a techno expert that was available to me at my fingertips was so sexy. You were the first man in over 16 years I had become over-the-top enamored with. It was like the first time I climaxed. In the past when I became transparent with someone, they were always part of the mental health community. I very seldom, if ever, showed my emotionally vulnerable side to a male companion or intimate friend.

Because I had been raised as a woman that you had to be strong at all times to be able to cover for your man. Matter of fact, in 11 years of marriage, my husband never saw me cry, and he witnessed me deliver three children. I cried in secret on the way to work after dropping off children to school or in the bathroom at 2:00 a.m.

I never saw my mate as strong enough to help me carry my emotional pain or capable of comforting me in it.

However, from day one, your soothing delivery of information calmed me like a person who has just had shock treatments to calm their mental anxiety. You unknowingly became my daily release. You did not ask for it or understand it. The fact that you put up with it made me drawn to you that much more. I realize that you are a very strong man to be able to put up with my emotional roller-coaster moments.

I had decided for the first time in my life I was going to be 100 percent transparent in a relationship from day one. Not wait the prescribed three to six months before the real me oozed out.

It has been an exhilarating journey. If when my love for you has not been reciprocated, your friendship and continued reassurance to me that you were a new fixture in my life was of great comfort.

I remember the day I gave you the reigns to navigate our relationship and you took them graciously. First thing you did was tell me to stop in the name of friendship and slow my roll. You asked, "What are you looking for from me?"

Yesterday, I spent the day recapping our friendship and realized how special you are as a friend to me. I feel you are not sexually attracted to me, although you enjoy my company. Even though I have enough sexual chemistry for both of us. LOL.

I now know I must seek other outlets for emotional dumping.

You don't have the time, energy or skill set to handle such a task. For using you that way, I apologize. I will become content with however much time I get to spend with you.

I will put on the brakes the vision of you as my life mate. I will be happy that you occasionally respond to my text and see me on periodic occasions.

I will begin the process of redefining what your presence in my life means. I know it will take time for me to let these intense feelings subside. So I ask for patience as I put you in the category for me you were never in: the category of friend.

For truly for me, you were love at first sight.

Sayonara

I have spent quality time thinking about you. What have I ever done but show you grace when you give me bullshit responses for lack of commitment and lying, deceitful behavior.

You asked what I wanted for Christmas. I told you and you promised me you would deliver. It has been over 60 days and nothing. When I was sick after dental surgery, you asked what kind of flowers and candy I liked. This was a mind game to make me think you cared about me. Yet once again, I got nothing, but you had brought it up.

So I know you know what to do, but I am not significant enough to you for you to invest in showing me you care about me because you don't. What you have done speaks volumes… Talk with no action is what you have given me.

On your birthday, I wanted you to know what having a partner who loved you felt like. I thought long and hard about what to get you. I even thought about having Junior's air flight a Vanilla Bean Cheesecake to you.

But by that time, I figured paying my bills was more important. Because I had already spent more money on you than any other man in my entire life. Yet Christmas… crickets, Valentine's Day… crickets, with the insult of it all being you showed me second-row tickets to the Oleta Adams concert at breakfast and told me you're buying them then, which was a lie.

The Ice Storm began on my birthday, which kept me from celebrating. I was so stupid and gullible, thinking you cared. You knew at breakfast you were not going to take me to the concert. You were so evil you notified me at a time too late for me to go by myself. I do not know why or how I became the chick that you make pay for all the brokenness from previous relationships. Yet I'm the one who showed you unconditional love. I finally got it.

You are only my IT expert. Because friends don't give out repeated hurt when shown love. So *sayonara* to what could have been a beautiful love story and friendship. Instead, now it is a business connection.

Darlin' No More

This morning I woke up and missed being referred to as Darlin'.

I wanted to reach out to you and give you words of encouragement as you instruct this weekend. I miss having someone I care about and love no longer being an intricate part of my life.

Yet being disrespected during important times in my life, I could no longer tolerate. But, as you know, absence from my life does not stop the feelings of loving you for the joy you brought to me in my life.

Thank you for teaching me patience and showing me I could fall in love again.

Even if the love was not reciprocated by you.

Missing the Idealistic Presence of You

Why do thoughts of you consume me?

Why do I miss your presence so?

When I think about all the times you ignored me and all the times you let me down, I know letting you go was the right thing.

But, babe, you made sure before I let you go, you planted your hooks in me.

I miss the soothing vocal cords of yours, which were capable of disarming me whenever I was stressed out.

I missed the capable way you listened as I rambled about my day.

I miss your intuitive insight into others' responses to actions I had taken. I miss holding you, caressing you, and most of all, I miss the completeness of myself. The completeness I felt when in your midst.

Every day I have to stop myself from calling you.

Every day I remind myself that if you pick up the phone, you may lash out and hurt me, and right now, I'm not emotionally strong enough to take the hurt.

Thank you for showing me new components in a relationship.

Thank you for letting me go without a fight.

Because whom you truly desire for a mate was someone other than me.

Mirage of Myself

I am in conflict with myself. In conflict for falling in love with a man who fell in love with someone else. I am in conflict battling to achieve the missions of my purpose. I am seeking something that for now should be on the back burner but I keep placing front and center.

I do not want to wallow in self-pity or empathy hell. I want to be that adult that can take the heartache and put it in a compartment and acknowledge it, yet move forward.

I want to then do what I do, accomplish the many tasks placed before me, bless others without longing for the presence of you.

Section Two

Dallas Rising

I met Dallas when I was twenty years old. We had a few things in common, including circulating in the same circles and had some affiliations through both being part of Black Greek organizations. Back then, we weren't interested in each other.

The premiere ladies' man, he was like an Arnold Schwarzenegger or Dwayne "The Rock" Johnson of his era. He was very athletically astute, had a black belt in karate, was a mathematical genius, grew up in the projects yet went to private school, had street sense, academic sense and spoke fluent French.

Much later, after I had been married with children and divorced, we had a chance encounter in my hometown grocery store. At that time, I was surprised because he still looked like the chiseled stallion he had been in his twenties.

He was surprised because I had just lost about 35 pounds and had gone through a rigorous exercise regimen, so I equally looked similar to when we first met, though we were both in our 40s.

We were both smitten at the possibilities…

Venus & Mars

The stars were aligned last night as you and I entered a new hemisphere together.

Sometimes great moments aren't recognized until years later. This moment's greatness had immediate significance.

There was an intensity of the moment. That said, the hour at hand is now.

Like two comets charging through space that collide in cosmic harmony instead of atmospheric chaos. What must be will be.

The respite we now take secures a permanent place in our destinies.

We now need each other more than we both want to accept, realize or understand.

The bind ties us together. The mental click has secured us in place.

When you hurt, I bleed. When your soul cries, my eyes are wet.

When your body craves of hunger, I replenish you.

We no longer have wills of our own. We march to the spontaneity of our own heart, even knowing we won't last forever. But what must be has to be for now.

To be deceitful or lie is not an option. To know the return investment is only known by a moment's sensation.

Yet destiny propels us, calls us to speed ahead as if euphoria awaits.

Purple Passion

The intensity of the moment.

The throbbing of our heartbeats as we hold our breath until our hearts beat as one.

The all-consuming synchronization of our physical bodies rocking, rotating in harmonious motion as we vibrated in unison to a whole new level.

The afterglow of our rendezvous blocked out the existence of anyone else but ourselves.

The peaceful slumber as we melted away in dreamland, and for once in my life, a dream had been fulfilled.

As we awaken to the dawn of a new day, we shared a new way of expressing our bond, and we actually did the impossible. We topped ourselves.

As we kissed our goodbyes, thoughts of purple passion surrendered to memories of black velvet swirls and wet tender juices that were so powerful, all the mystique and facade were eliminated.

All that remained were raw, sensual intensity of joyous escapades of pure, unadulterated lovemaking.

The Voice

Your voice continues to mesmerize me and continues to cause me to be oblivious of all the other things around me.

The tenderness in your delivery of appropriate responses to random acts of kindness and the humbleness that you constantly strive to maintain put you in an elite class of "sincere friends."

Friends that you can call after the midnight hour and will receive a warm reception instead of, "What the hell?!"

The voice you project has a soothing effect on my psyche. The voice that transfers concerns of mine into a workable plan of action to resolve the issue that is most pressing at the moment.

The voice that puts his own conflict on hold to deal with mine. The voice of my sincere #1 friend, YOU.

Pity the Brother

So, you opted to have a pity party. Poor little pitiful me.

The white folks don't love me no mo'.

I am experiencing something akin to writer's block. Stop the world, I want to get off.

I can't take this snag in my professional creativity.

What's a Brother to do?

My nicely made plans to vacate and flee the scene for warm pastures and greater financial and professional opportunity has hit a giant snag. I can't get out of my lease.

I don't like my job anymore.

The new gig that was supposed to start on the first of the month hasn't arrived yet. Alas, I don't know why it hasn't been delivered Special Delivery. Hey, I would have even paid the COD fee at this point.

And speaking of a Love Life, poor, sad, pitiful me.

What's a Brother to do when his libido no longer matches his ego? When he has a woman in the South planning the future of a lifetime. And a woman in the Midwest planning an experience of a lifetime.

Poor me. Please don't cry for me.

As you can all see how distressed and horrible my life is. Who could possibly endure what I'm enduring?

And speaking of jobs, who could possibly endure the professional responsibilities I must conquer daily.

Who would want a job that:

A. Expects you to do just what you were hired for and isn't open to you going beyond that;
B. Allows you to express your community involvement and civic duty by only granting two professional development days annually;
C. Sets deadlines for project completion but doesn't give you a written reprimand when you let them pass?

Hey world, stop.

I need to get off.

My life is so destitute.

Don't all you homeless, one-paycheck-from-being-homeless people feel sorry for me?

I am only able to pay my bills.

I haven't been able to invest in the 401k plan at work in six months.

Okay, enough about me; how is your day?

Dilemma

You waltzed into my life with a price on your head.

You swept me off my feet and promised to make my dreams come true and delivered. Yet the one dream of you was already sold to a previous bidder. Since you are a man of your word, you belong to the bidder. If you renege on the bidder, you renege on yourself.

For what is a man without his word?

Well, you offered me my one moment to follow my heart and not my mind. In fact, you encouraged me to go with the flow and risk total emotional annihilation. For yours and my selfish desires of sensual ecstasy.

Yet when the owner of you whisks you away from me, you two will have each other and a lifetime to create new fantasies to wipe away all memories of me. I'll have to once again pick up my broken heart and find some superglue strong enough to heal the wound.

I'll have to find a diversion for tears and conquer my weakness of allowing myself to be vulnerable once again.

Knowing, as I have always known, to be a woman and be vulnerable is to be hurt and set yourself up to feeling used.

But you did not use me. Hopefully during this time of recollection, I'll erase the flaw within my being that attracts me to persecution relationships. Maybe your purpose was to assist me in realizing I'm capable of having a loving and monogamous relationship.

Therefore, I have two choices: to settle for less or settle for no relationship at all, with you.

Agony and Ecstasy

The pain of your existence was acutely felt.

The agony that your spirit is experiencing as your mental psyche volleys back and forth with past visions of "I am the man" and "to be or not to be."

I hold the answer, which is different from Shakespeare asking the question. Has been replaced with newfound doubts of "Has my entire mystique been a facade?"

Have I wasted all this time, energy, skill and preparedness on an unrealistic ideal?

Your feeling of inadequacy penetrated my consciousness and left me feeling strange and more sure-footed, realizing, yes, I can make it.

Your heart slipping up and showing me your innermost private sanctum of vulnerability let me know how truly blessed I was.

For few women, if any, have witnessed such an obvious display of humanness and Homo sapiens frailty from you as I did in those few precious moments of rediscovery.

For once I felt like Lois Lane with Superman or Tracy with the Black Panther. Rest assured, your breach of honor did not go unappreciated or un-cherished.

As long as I live, I will remember that "gift" that you gave me.

You may have the pictures, but I witnessed and captured a piece of your soul. Thank you.

Alpha Omega, Omega Alpha

I don't do endings well.

The Scriptures say the first shall be last and the last shall be first. And so it is with us.

You told me the ending before the beginning.

Alas, no one to blame, no shame to hide upon. No betrayal to cling to.

I must stand up and face it like a woman. Because that I am W.O.M.A.N.

Some things you avoid like the plague. For me, it was spontaneity.

There was this deep-seated inner consciousness that told me you can't handle that.

You need props, baby.

As the New Year dawned, I envisioned a new me.

I experienced a new I could see. For a fleeting moment, I believed I could fly. So to you, I said, "Watch me soar."

Now I must return to the floor and tread a tad bit lightly through an open door. But you made me feel so free, so released, unleashed; you were my liberator.

As a wise friend once told me, please don't make me release this bitch inside of me because even I'm scared of her.

Well, she's been released.

My body wants you, My mind drinks of you. My heart beats of you.

Every waking moment consumes you.

Please give me a fleeting respite from your passionate touch.

Take away the addictive juices of your love so I may focus on reality once again.

My Heart Is Black

Black like the deep charcoals that forever fire up the grill and burn endlessly into the night long after the last "stake" has left the grill.

What's at stake now? Is it financial freedom, professional independence or creative expertise exercised in a venue of your own undoing?

Can you walk that walk, talk that talk and smack that mack, Jack?

Can you feel the wheel of the new car you drive, or are you too afraid to close your eyes and put the car on autopilot?

Hey, tell me, what's at stake now?!

AutoCadding

I'm CAD-in' for you, baby, and I don't mean maybe.

AutoCad, French curves, specs watch me genuflect.

Precision, concise, can't second guess twice. Accuracy is your specialty.

Minute details lead to perfection. When you bum rush it, you can't trust it.

Then you take a chance that you hit a snag. Must check it with AutoCad.

For the dimensions and suspension curve to be just right, 5/8 of an inch, it can't be off.

Like precision-tuned, the power's in the hands to envision what the mind pretends.

You got it, you know it.

Take care, don't blow it and get tacky, wacky and careless instead of Mr. Concise, whom I also think you may be much too nice for the fucked-up industry in which you must create.

Don't let their pollution hibernate in your soul, for it will stagnate and pollute the you of you's.

I Can Hear You Smiling

As you answered the phone and realized I was on the other end, I could hear the changing intonations of your vocal cords.

I could hear you smiling.

I hear the joy in your voice. I can visualize your cheeks rising and expanding in a beautiful smile that captivates all who see you.

I hear you smiling in the comfort of peace in your spirit and voice, as you speak of having a new sense of direction and purpose, as you chart your future path.

Oh the joy you gave me as I could feel the confidence and contentment you have for yourself.

Today, I Can Hear You Smiling.

I Can Make It Rain

I CAN MAKE IT RAIN, just by my awesome presence.

I can make the dumb talk and the paralyzed walk with a raised eyebrow and a quirky smile.

Trust me, I CAN MAKE IT RAIN.

Because my word is solid like a rock, and I am trustworthy to a fault.

Doors and opportunities abound at my disposal.

I CAN MAKE IT RAIN. I don't talk sh*t.

I speak things into existence due to my steadfast commitment and honor-bound duty and visions of being a responsible citizen.

I CAN MAKE IT RAIN.

I don't have to inflict pain on you physically because I can on any given day outthink you mentally.

I CAN MAKE IT RAIN buckets of water if you cross my path and intentionally misstep. You will witness and experience Hell on Earth.

I CAN MAKE IT RAIN. Don't ever underestimate me again. 'Cause, sister, I CAN MAKE IT RAIN.

Did I make myself plain?

Intensive Thought

As I wake up,

As I sigh,

Thoughts of your smile,

Your deep soothing voice,

Your tall powerful stride,

Gives me fantasies of You.

Straddling me and taking me to a new place,

As you enter my special place

That is waiting for You.

Waiting in anticipation,

Due to all the wolf tickets you have sold regarding

How expertly capable you are at rocking my world.

Intensive Thought: what meeting You has caused me to do.

Spending way too much time thinking about You.

Sexy Vocal Cords

Those sexy vocal cords have done a number on my heart.

The tenderness in your voice when you are speaking words of comfort when you try to appease and quiet the raging storm, which is the aftermath of a hard day stressed out by other people's anxieties.

Your sexy vocal cords reach down into the innermost places and let me know I'm alive and well.

You give me a new reason to hope and cope with the daily strife of life.

She Butter

SHE BUTTER, she be the off-yellow smooth, silky wet, yet warm to the touch of loveliness that glides as I smother her all over my existence.

Like African oil, her body coils in response to my masterful stroke as I gently massage her stroke after stroke into my being.

Man, SHE be the BUTTER to my bread. It's too late; I've already lost my head. Her soothing fluids have already cascaded through my pores, softening the once hardened calluses that protrude out of my skin like a coat of arms to my masculinity and toughness.

SHE BUTTER, at the instant she announces her presence, the room illuminates. Men involuntarily gyrate to adjust their stance so other women with them can't notice the sudden dance that just started in their pants at her entrance.

SHE BUTTER, just what I want a woman to feel like.

SHE BUTTER, just what a woman should do: make you feel warm, secure and totally absorbed in you all's existence.

Hey, that woman, SHE be BUTTER to me!

Intimate Sessions

The softness of your touch.

The essence of masculinity that assaulted my senses.

The warm feel of your body next to mine.

The tenderness of your kisses as you explored my mouth with the tenderness reserved for neophyte initiation.

The timeless effort you take to make me come to new heights and dimensions of ecstasy.

Your pain was intense, but your perseverance was so sincere as to be a precious memory.

Your revelation, which flowed so effortlessly from your lips, was like a drunken man who unknowingly blurts out the truth for he is too intoxicated to process a lie. Truly the trip of this week was the trip-up when I could truly say "checkmate."

As I parted from your sweetness, throughout the day, I glowed and glistened inside from the soothing security and comfort of your touch.

For a man who shot blanks, I gained warmth and intensity in intimacy I haven't experienced in a long time.

Thank you ever so much for yet another spectacular performance.

Just Being Nasty

When I think of the first time we made love, you sexed me till all my guards went down along with my drawers.

I remember the release and the freedom and reckless abandonment of letting it all hang out as we reached for climax after climax, achieving the goal of JUST BEING NASTY.

No one else in the world existed as we both slipped out of consciousness to achieve the unthinkable. A climax where truly no one was there but us. We could not have heard the phone, doorbell or smoke alarm.

For we were on Fire, achieving and believing the best thing in Life at that moment was JUST BEING NASTY.

Logitech

Alright, you finally made it plain, or as you so succinctly stated, "Crystal."

According to your Logitech formula of the specs for a perfect woman, I meet all the logistical computations. However, due to a reprogramming error in your hard drive, our systems are no longer compatible, Alas, you thought that by now you would have received and formulated the microchip that would have somehow made our systems with such similar software a match made in heaven.

But hey, even though Gateway is a great computer, so is Macintosh.

Both are great systems, but unfortunately, they aren't compatible.

As a great singer once said, "If it don't fit, don't force it."

I Hear You

I heard it in your voice.

I won't call.

I heard it in your heart. It's over now.

Forgive me for calling,

But I had to know, and you told me so.

First with your heart,

And then with your mind.

And finally with your words.

Thank you for allowing me to feel the you I knew, not by words but by touch, by feel, by mental heartstrings, by intuitive connectedness.

Mr. Blank, Blank, you will be hard to replace.

Miles Apart

Sounds of a distant past,
melodies that strum a beat and
a pathway to my heart—
thoughts of you are but a memory,
like a song that suddenly
pops into my head
during the middle of the day.

Sounds of a recent present,
melodies that repeat the beat
through life experiences and pseudo suitors,
or he mimics some stance or gesture
that has the fabric of you.

Sounds of a millennium future,
melodies that echo the ingenuity and finesse
of my character and strength that,
for us, can be directly attributed to
our unique encounter and immersion
of a mental and spiritual kind.

Sounds that incorporate the support and agony
our association has brought to the other,
melodies that play a song
few men are strong enough
to experience—
and walk away from—
and never look back.

Sounds whose very presence affirms our vitality,
melodies that confirm our gift to stand out
and be the core and center of any encounter

Thoughts of you have reached a crescendo
and now are so much a part of me that
the you have ceased to be.

Mr. No, No, No, No, No

MR. NO, NO, NO, NO, NO, with your smooth suave rap and the tender vibrations that course through my body at the initial seconds of your touch.

You energize me and pour on your charm… and tantalize me with electric shock kisses that have the power of giving me an instant lube job.

MR. NO, NO, NO, NO, NO, who is used to being MR. YES, YES, YES, YES, YES, for it's hard for a woman to resist your charms.

MR. NO, NO, NO, NO, NO is what you will be for me now. Because I can't afford to tumble into your clutches and have you march on my heart like King marched on Washington.

But for a moment, I can reminisce about your kisses à la electric and the shock treatments your fingers work as you massaged all those special places.

For my reality, the warning sign is glaring bold neon orange.

But MR. NO, NO, NO, NO, NO, if asked am I happy to have experienced you, the answer would be a resounding YES, YES, YES, YES, YES!

Robber Baron

Your encouragement means a lot. Your opinion has great validity. Your body reminds me just how much of a difference one can make.

Your touch reminds me of just how powerful your aura is.

Your feel reaches deep down into the recesses of my anatomy and cries for redemption.

Your kiss starts the vibration from my saliva glands and paralyzes my jaws as the shock waves move to encompass all the private spaces of my existence.

As you kiss me from head to toe and introduce your tongue to all my special intimate spaces, intense heat and desire overcome me as I become physically afraid that my heart can't last if I totally give in to the experience.

As you stroke my hair and whisper words of encouragement, the tough skin wall of protection melts, and once again, my soul surrenders under your spell. As I realize my body has been robbed once again by a Baron of a fellow, who after he flees into the darkness of the night, I feel empty and incomplete as I try to compete for an encore of his performance.

And I learned the hard way, 99 and ½ won't do unless it's you!

Sweet Serenity

Sweet Serenity that calms my soul and wills me whole after a bitch of a day.

Sweet Serenity, you have engulfed me and taken control. I can feel the peace flowing throughout my existence willing the stress and strain away.

Sweet Serenity, take me, take me to that peaceful place that blends with the now peaceful space of my existence.

Sweet Serenity that calms my soul and makes me whole.

It gives me the strength to face another day.

Take a Minute

Just take a minute to step in someone else's shoes.

It may give you a clue to their existence.

It may give you a clue if for a moment you focused on something other than you.

Just for a minute, let God step in it and give you a peek at someone else having a moment of need. Won't you heed their call, or is it all about the almighty me?!

You need to get with the program and revamp the "me" to the "we." For "me" is awfully lonely.

Just take a minute to step into someone else's shoes, and when you need a helping hand, you would have already paid your dividends into your insurance plan. Understood?

Tasty Love

The soft yet firm touch of your lips, as they caressed and molded in a harmonious dance with mine. The unique taste and feel of your mouth.

The jolt of excitement felt as our tongues participated in a slow dance of introduction before going on a spontaneous adventure of intoxication, lust and passion.

Tasty Love… Thank you for the experience of you.

The Joneses

Baby, I've got the Joneses for your love. I pray to God above to hold you, keep you safe for my keeping. Now I have lonely nights where just sleeping escapes me. For thoughts of your sensations and overall presentation dominate my mind. I hope you are doing fine. I miss you so much this time. More than ever before. Baby, I can't let you go. Though I know you are so unsure of where I stand in your flight plan, I just don't want to understand life, love, without you.

Baby, I've got the Joneses for your love.

Thoughts of You

Thoughts of you linger throughout my consciousness.

Thoughts of how good you feel inside of me.

Thoughts of how you call me in terms of endearment.

Thoughts of how our minds clicked in synchronization where I could start a sentence…

And we would simultaneously finish it.

Thoughts of you linger throughout my consciousness and possess all my open spaces.

Thoughts of you consume my heart and soul as I volley to retake control.

Thoughts of you without me are part of my existence that I find hard to see.

Even though you left my place, when I wake up, I see your face.

I have to shake my head to see it's just the mirage inside of me.

Thoughts of you linger throughout my consciousness, and I wonder, was I so easy to forget?

Are you now getting your needs met? For you met mine when you were here once upon a time.

Thoughts of you linger throughout my consciousness.

Today

Today you came.

Today you came to me and with me. Today you came because I called.

Today you came and reaffirmed what you mean to me.

Today you came,

Yet left in an instant.

Today you came. But if my tomorrows mirror my yesterdays,

In my heart I know,

You are already gone.

Whipping Stick Love

You've got that whipping stick love.

Where the rage comes up when there's too many days and nights without you.

You've got that whipping stick love when I'm with you.

I don't want you ever to leave me.

If you head for the door, that's what the whipping stick is for.

To smack you back into my bed.

Boy, you inside my head.

Don't be misled; instead, it's just that you got that whipping stick love.

Love that makes you want more.

You got that whipping stick love that makes me love you forever more.

Wounded Warrior

The dream and the challenge of captivating a boundless entity was too great to pass up.

I pulled out the stops and gave it all.

I had no avail.

The battle of the two worlds had begun. The only wounded is me.

I'm now physically maimed from the emotional strain of the battle cry of my heart.

As I try to forge a new entity out of the remnants of my existence,

The question remains.

Will I ever have so much fun in battle again?

You Are Genuine

You have honest eyes. You have a determined heart. You have the voice of conviction. You have gifts to share with the world.

You Are Genuine.
It takes time to know just where you are and fill your space.
It takes time before you know the path or your destiny.

You Are Genuine.
You will be fine.
Just stay prayed up, and He will lift you up.

Memories

Memories of the you I wanted you to be.

Memories of the look of anticipation of what we could have been.

Memories that show a distortion of the truth, clouded by fantasies that took on a life of its own.

Memories of good, raw, gut-wrenching climactic experiences, which allowed us to release whatever needed to be released.

Memories of holding each other, arms intertwined, welcoming daybreak from peaceful slumber.

Memories of you and my entire physical existence as I vibrated and smacked, awaiting your touch so my body fluids can flow in reckless abandonment.

Memories of wanting you, and needing you, to fulfill a need. To fill up a space inside of me so I could feel whole and connected to someone or something for just a moment.

Memories of lustful desires unfulfilled or that surpassed my expectations.

Memories, it appears, that's all we have left of the us that is no more.

Memories, as they fade, will time be kind to them? Or will the memory exist as another failed relationship that began with so much love and promise, yet dissolved due to deceit and greed?

Memories, the substance that holds the mental history of our past, which propels us toward a bright future, hoping one day through the experiences of our past, we can finally get it right; the memory becomes a daily reality of relationship gladness, for memories linger on.

Since You Died

Since you died, I have nowhere to hide my pain.

Since you died, I feel empty inside.

Thou you were tormented here on earth,

I knew your worth.

Your presence instilled a sense of peace.

You presence filled a void.

Since you died, I must acknowledge the loneliness I feel.

Since you died, I realize that no matter how I tried, I could not be all things to you.

There was still a void I often tried to ignore that you needed and I couldn't fulfill.

Death truly lets us know how powerless we are.

No matter how much money, honey, we have.

No matter how hard we love, when God above says "come home," we are left alone.

We are without the physical presence of the one we adored.

Since you died, I've been forced to go inside myself.

Never again will I doubt the power of God for a fleeting second. For he let me love you.

He let me have a relationship with you that superseded all the others. Yet he still had the power to take it away in an instant, without warning.

Since you died, a lot of changes I've made.

Now things have to be more on my terms.

Now things must make me happy, not make me sad. I have little to no tolerance for relationship pain. I value me more, not less.

I no longer look for someone else to define my happiness. I look for me to define who I will be.

No longer will I get lost in love again and struggle to find me when it's all over, you see.

Since you died, a new me has emerged inside, stronger, bolder and older, with fierce determination to live each day to the fullest, kicking and screaming and enjoying every moment just the way I want to do.

One day at a time, learning and embracing our unique collaboration.

Yet open to experience the new ones to come.

Knowing with blessed assurance, God sees all and knows all, and He is the one truly running it. We just run around in it.

Since you died, I have a new woman inside me, screaming to get out and right the wrongs of this world.

I now know I don't have forever to exist. I must make every day count.

Since you died, new friends have come and gone. Old friends try to hang on, but I now have little tolerance for their insecurities.

Since you died, I no longer care what others think unless they influence my livelihood; we know it shouldn't, but since when did "shouldn't" have any power?

Since you've been gone, I still long for your presence and such…

I miss you so much yet can't think of a thing I needed to say that wasn't said. It must all be in my head that I still need you.

Yet I know what I must do and have done.

I've truly moved on… But you were such a different one. You just can't be replaced or erased from my memory.

Dedicated to my fiancé, who passed three days after he proposed to me…

Grief Consumes Me

Lord, what must I do?

You brought into my life the radiant energy that made me laugh, smile and beam like a light bulb that never loses its light.

On our bad days, when we just could not be on that one accord, living without each other seemed like a possibility.

You would touch his heart so he would touch mine. I would receive wonderful makeup gifts and a thousand reasons why the issue of dissension wasn't as important as our first moment of unification. Lord, now that's physically gone from me; how am I to make it through the day with a smile of hope and love on my face?

I miss his warm embrace…

I miss the smell of him… fresh and raw and funky at the break of dawn after he opened me up like the morning sun and filled my open space with the essence of him.

I miss the smell of him coming out of the bathroom after a shower in the early morning, and I miss how the scent of Angel for Men body gel mixed with his natural essence.

I miss the smell of him on the linen after he got out of bed.

As I changed the sheets, I would sometimes lift them up so I could smell him and envision the taste of him again. I miss the mortal man I could pray with as a prayer partner in one accord.

I miss the debates that began as arguments and ended with passionate, competitive sparring sessions. To see who could out do the other in the passionate makeup sessions.

I miss the warmth of lips that knew just when to part to make me open up my heart to him.

Lord, how can I feel joy, laughter and the witness between my legs again after a passionate night in the sack helped release the stress and the drama of the day?

Lord, I know you won't put more on us that we can bear, and I know that I must let go and let God and that you remove one thing to bring something greater and more fulfilling into my life.

But Lord, I am going to need your help to be able to see this.

For right now, my past represents my better days. And my present a bleak presentation of agony that multiplies instead of subsides.

Lord, please help me to crave you and not the him that will never be here again.

Help me to see and relish the blessings I've had and give me the ability to recognize the blessings that are to come.

Because right now, grief consumes me.

Section Three

Raw Sensuality

These poems were written in some instances in paying homage to my role as a therapist and others' relationship dilemmas and navigating to a healthy outcome, even if the outcome was leaving.

Some have to do with relationships I was in, like with a guy (Wolf) who liked me and had been married for close to 45 years, but he kept hounding me. It was insulting, disgusting and horrible for him to try and holler at me. He wanted his cake and to eat it too… He looked like such a nice person, but he was a dog.

Why would I want to have a relationship with a married man? Why?

"Single Ain't Shit" is a frustration anthem… not because I want it to be, but because it's real, though many of us don't want it to be.

Don't we all want someone with whom we are evenly yoked intellectually and also have romantic chemistry with? But how many times have we settled because "I Can't Lay Down with My Checking Account"?

Single Ain't Shit

Single, available, seasoned, not old. Just wanting some respite from the mundane existence of sleep, work and preparation for work. Just want someone capable of breaking the monotony and introducing some spice to my life. 'Cuz hanging out in bars trying to meet stars looks and feels like a meat market. I'm single, available and seasoned, not old. Make no mistake about it—old I'm not.

I'm single, available and seasoned. Is that the reason I'm all alone? No man to call my own, having a house, not a home. Unsure how to undo this wall of confidence and self-assuredness. Undo just enough to let someone in and we build it back up again.

I wish I could stop the pain, the pain of aloneness.

Dinner for one, movie ticket for one, somehow this road I'm travelin' on must be undone.

BECAUSE BEING SINGLE AIN'T SHIT!

I Want a Man

Yes, I want a man, but you must understand, I have standards!

I don't want no crackhead or stupid man who brings more grief than relief.

I don't want no man without a home.

I'd rather be alone. I already got kids of my own.

Yes, I want a man, not one whose past is so checkered he will never see the "right" of day.

Yes, I want a man. One I can stand by and is capable of standing by me, and even picking me up and carrying me through.

I want a man; understand?

I Need a Man That Can Put It Down

I am a multifaceted woman who can do more than one thing well at a time. That's why I need a man to be around.

You know, my own personal handyman to fix what I can't.

A man who understands I enjoy being soft, feminine and strong.

In order for us to get along, I need a man to be around that can operate the hammer in his hand.

That can fix my plumbing and mow my lawn when it gets overgrown.

Now I hope you understand.

I Want a Man I Can Take Outside

I want a man I can take outside and expose him to all the beautiful, mind-boggling, intellectual experiences that are the foundation of solutions to our people's ills.

I want a man I can take outside, and we can jointly network toward creating a better future.

I want a man I can take outside in the world of diversity and he not be intimidated by conversing with someone male or female who makes double his salary.

I want a man I can take outside and feel happiness inside at the pride I feel for being with a man who is emotionally, intellectually, spiritually my peer. Who hears what I hear and we march to the same beat, even if sometimes we go in a different direction to get there.

Please GOD, Send Me a Man I Can Take Outside!!!

What I Want from You

I want, first and foremost, a friend I can be transparent with.

Second, I want to be taken seriously and not viewed as a delusional woman. Third, I want our relationship to grow and not stagnate. Fourth, I need you to check in with me every other day. I know I have an extra presence. No matter how much I try to dim my light, it surfaces. I have read your stop signs. I am trying to reel myself in and just be content and thankful that God has gifted me with a new best male friend.

What You Want From Me

What you want from me is yet to be determined. Honest and being authentic is on your list. However, I do not think your brilliant-as-can-be persona was prepared for how brutally honest I am. As time goes on, I'm sure you will let me know what you want from me. And I will definitely let you know if I will accept the challenge and deliver.

Lying Eyes

I'm the one you come to with those lying eyes.

I'm the one other woman your wife despises.

I'm the one you vent to about her alleged deficiencies,

But spare me your marital drama, if you please.

It's been long enough for you to make a clean break.

For if it's really that bad, divorce her, for heaven's sake.

I see the truth now; I was just too young to understand.

I fell in love with a boy but not a man.

I loved and believed those lying eyes,

Becoming a woman other God-fearing women despise.

Now the time has come for you to go.

Let the door hit you where the good Lord split you and take your shit and go.

I've had enough of your weak excuses of why we will never be.

I refuse to be a part of this tragedy anymore, you see.

I see the truth now; I was just too young to understand.

I fell in love with a boy, but now my mind, body and soul requires

A man!!!!

One to Put It Down and One to Be Around

I need a man who can put it down.

Not downtown, but put it down in my private domain.

I need a man who can take charge, yet not bully.

I need a man who does not need an instruction manual.

A man who can be, for me, fully equipped and operational.

Wolf in Sheep's Clothing

Hey, you, Wolf in Sheep's Clothing…

Why do you attempt to pursue that which you have no rightful heir to? Hey, you, Wolf in Sheep's Clothing, do you have a conscience? Doesn't it bother you that you made vows before God to Love, Honor and cherish another, yet you are consistently all up on my spot? Why do you men have double standards? When a woman pursues you, she's loose. But when you pursue her, she's all that and a bag of chips. Hey, you, Wolf in Sheep's Clothing, you appear to be a man of character and poise, but I don't have time for any noise that is going in any direction other than Friendship. A home wrecker, I am not. A good friend, I've gotten awards for being that! Hey, you, Wolf in Sheep's Clothing, can I give you some advice? Slow down. Reassess what you have. And do what you can to keep it. Every battery needs to be recharged. So, recharge yours.

Do something different. Plan a weekend getaway for just the two of you to a winery or bed & breakfast. Give her a wad of money to go shopping and actually take time to listen to where she wants your relationship to go in the upcoming years. Schedule a massage for two so both of you can relax and unwind before you talk. Have some wine or sparkling cider chilled and present her with chocolate strawberries, which you will feed to her.

Hey, you, Wolf in Sheep's Clothing, remember God joined you two together for a reason. And as long as you two have been together, it's lasted more than a season. So, rekindle those fires that are lightly dimmed. Rekindle from within and don't seek happiness outside of your stratosphere. You have spent plenty of time out of the house and not enough time at home. Working two, three jobs is fine if your goal in life is to receive a Provider Medal. But when do you have time to enjoy the fruits of your labor?

Both of you have changed. Your physical makeup isn't what it used to be and neither is hers. You are away so much, the two of you are now different people because you have so few of the same experiences that coincide. Are you trying to die and leave her a stash of cash to spend on the new honey that doesn't work but can give her all the quality time she needs if the price is right?

Readjust your schedule to include quality time weekly where the cell phone is turned off, the TV is turned off, and try to listen to the melodious voices of each other and do something spontaneous and new with each other. Don't try to bring me or someone else in a situation that's supposed to be a pair (with two people) and turn it into a triangle (with three people).

Ben—Done

Add today as a day I've thought about you, the vision and the perception of you and me together. All week I thought of you and had to restrain myself from reaching out for fear you would think I was stalking you, since the need to connect with you was so overpowering.

Today I couldn't take it anymore and texted you to inquire if I could see you. You said yes and I was there.

Today we were reunited once again. All communication between you, toward me, was "you" centered. I waited and waited for the conversation to include me. Did not happen!

Today I want to thank you for destroying the illusion of your charismatic persona. It is only charismatic if viewed from a distance. It is toxic narcissism if you get up close and try to get personal.

Thank you for allowing me to see that being in a relationship with you is a relationship of one instead of a relationship of two.

Thank you for letting me know you live in the realm of I and me—not us and we.

Thank you for the very early wake-up call. You did not let me fall into your trap of perceiving your crap was legit. You never had the chance to break my heart.

Thank you for the premature ejaculation of my one-sided chemistry connection, which just got disconnected.

Thank you for being you and letting me know you don't have time for me. You only have time for thee in your flight plan.

Thank you, Ben, for the clear perspective.

If I Could Slow You Down, I'd Show You Something

Girl, if I could slow you down, I'd show you something.

If you slow yo' roll girl, I'll make it worth yo' while.

Man, stop talking all this here trash to a sister. If I could make you look upon me as an equal and not as a child that fulfills your every whim, we would not even be having this conversation.

Slow me down for what? Are you capable of paying all my bills and yours and still live at your house instead of trying to creep all up in mine?

Are you willing to let me retire from my job and slow down and catch a breath and you keep me in the lifestyle I'm accustomed to while I take a breather to find myself?

Are you willing to admit to yourself you like my independence enough to admire it, not try to squash it for your selfish, dominant desires?

So, my question is, do you really want a "slow woman," or are you looking for a challenge that will make you stand erect and know that you must keep your game in check or I will say checkmate on your ass?

So, my question is, do you need me to slow down for a while just so you can catch up to my speed?

Is It Spring or Are You Cold?

Hey, are you really and truly looking for a relationship with give and take, instead of "bip, bam, thank you ma'am"?

For fulfilling a need, or is it, "But I've got too many other shores to sail my ship in before the cold, cold winter sets in."

I'll say it again another way: "Are you looking for a relationship, or are you just trying to get warm?"

You know, hibernate in the warm softness of my buxom fold until the winter thaws and spring rushes in with the wind, sunshine and rain. And you begin to have the visuals of a tall, thin skinny in a mini. Visions of strapless tops and daisy dukes instead of Bertha Butt that can only be displayed as you get laid and viewed for your eyes only.

As I said, "Is it spring or are you cold?"

I'm a Nurturer, Not a Nurse

Good morning to all you people who thirst for my goodness and mercy.

Good morning to you. I bring you today's news regarding my perspective.

I Am a Nurturer, Not a Nurse.

I relish and enjoy helping you navigate through the turbulent valleys of your emotional low points. I champion solutions that cause you to make better decisions and experience less strife. Not make the same mistakes on multiple occasions.

I assist you and am there for you because I genuinely care about you.

Not because I'm the sucker for the month.

I can take rejection; I can take you are not my type.

What I refuse to take is you blatantly using me under the premise that you care.

You only want me there because I appear to be the best person to fulfill your need.

When the time comes and God strikes you down physically and Visiting Nurses become a priority in your life, you call me.

Feeding my mind with declarations of how special I am.

You thinking that will make me want to volunteer to do what Visiting Nurses do for a monetary stipend. You thinking I would gladly do it for free.

Not realizing that I had the Insight to realize that in our past, you only were with me to use me.

I'm a Nurturer, Not a Nurse.

I Can't Lay Down with My Checking Account

Daylight dawns… another morning comes without your arms around me welcoming in a new day.

Momma raised me that if you don't stand for something, you will fall for anything.

With strong convictions and character, I told you "no money, no honey." A man without a job and who by all appearances doesn't appear to be working overtime to find one can't spend his nights rocking me in the sheets, whispering sweet, sensuous thoughts of passion in my ear.

And then as morning breaks, I'm the only one going to work.

Yet my body craves you. Even though my mind knows you don't have the standards to be my even yoke.

The chemistry with you was no joke. And my heart gave me an instant message text: you can't lay down with your checking account.

Dingwat

Don't go. Please stay. Please don't run away and never come back.

Please don't break my heart again.

I can't continue to learn to trust the same man over and over again. Don't sour my existence of love, happy endings and second chances.

For once, let my misguided faith in humanity yield a positive outcome.

Don't let our relationship become another statistic of failed promises.

Please don't go. Please stay in a physical sense. In an emotional sense, I can't seem to let go of the hope and dream that you will one day see I am the best thing that ever happened to you.

Now, please go away if you don't plan on ever making an honest woman of me. You be strong enough to let me go so eventually the pain will subside. I can then learn to feel whole again and mend the broken spaces of my existence that try to make me settle for a partial man instead of a whole one.

Please, for once, think of someone other than you. Help me be all that I can be by leaving now!

Depression

Depression... When the anguish of everyday existence merges one day into the other, and it appears no relief is in sight.

The dark gloom cloud of Depression has arrived.

When visuals of asses and elbows all contorted for your benefit just can't shake the blue funk, Depression is here.

But Depression doesn't have to reign supreme.

You must think and, by willpower, guts and prayer, will the reality you want into existence.

You wake up and say a prayer of Thanksgiving and rejoice for the gift of the future existence that is to come and approach your day like it's already bright and sunny, with no gloom on the horizon.

You must use the power of Positive Thought to overcome negative energy.

You're a Snake in the Ass

You're a snake, snake, snake, snake in the ass. Not to be confused with a snake in the grass.

You're a snake, snake, snake, snake in the ass. Ooooh ooooh, it's much more than personal.

You were blessed with looks and charm, though you have none.

You roll like a thief, a thief in the night. You strike in the dark and out of clear sight.

You're a snake, snake, snake, snake in the ass, wearing business suits yet exhibiting no class.

You're a snake, snake, snake, snake in the ass. Ooooh, you've got no class.

You've got degrees but no integrity. You lie, cheat and steal so unnecessarily.

You're a snake, snake, snake, snake in the ass. You'd sell your own momma for a piece of ass.

You're a snake, snake, snake, snake in the ass. Ooooh, you've got no class.

You speak with a forked tongue, and your word can't be trusted. If people believe what you say, they soon find out they will be busted. You don't care about others, only yourself. Ooooh, you're a pitiful sight.

You're a snake, snake, snake, snake in the ass. One of these days, justice will arrive and corral your ass. It will make you pay for all the strife you have inflicted on others' lives. Hopefully she dishes it out as cold as you have because you have no heart.

You're a snake, snake, snake, snake in the ass. Not to be confused with a snake in the grass.

You're a snake, snake, snake, snake in the ass. Ooooh ooooh, it's much more than personal.

Fleabag Reality Check

Have you ever had a fantasy where you meet this person and the physical presence of him is awesome?

Have you ever had a fantasy about how you and this dream man, ultra-specimen of a man, would be until… all the energy and mental space given to the real-life dream is shattered by reality?

Instead of the vocal ministrations echoed over the telecommunications, Oh baby, I want you with a vengeance… I just want the chance to pamper you, give you a full body massage and ease all the tension in your life.

Baby, you need a quiet, intimate retreat for two.

Have you experienced ice… Oh, by the way, baby, do you have a feather? Can you surprise my eyes with a unique playsuit for my eyes only?

The reality is, instead of an intimate, romantic getaway at the Ritz-Carlton, you are escorted to a down-and-out hideaway in the hood.

Instead of plush towels and matching terry cloth robes, you got a ghetto hand towel and wash rag.

Instead of a satellite dish or cable, you get AM radio and TV, if you are able.

And instead of being able to concentrate on the ministration of seduction, you are mortified and petrified with the shock and revelation that you are with another guy, a squirrel just trying to get a nut.

Stop It!

Stop It! Can't you see the terror in my eyes?

Stop It! When did domination of my soul become your relationship goal?

Stop It! You profess you love me.

Yet whenever I utter an independent thought, you terrorize me.

Whenever I operate in a manner that increases my self-esteem and builds my character, you knock me down like dominoes.

Oh, the blows I've had to sustain.

Emotional pain of belittling me in front of my children.

Being kicked and dragged behind closed doors.

Stop It! You don't want a mate to cherish.

You want a lap dog you can train or a puppet you can manipulate and pull all the strings.

Stop IT! NO more trying to erase me so I can be this sick interpretation of what you want me to be.

Stop It! I'm grown. Already been raised.

Stop It! Don't let my strength be the object of my annihilation.

Stop It! Grown weary of the threats.

Stop It! Grown tired of feeling dead inside because you have stripped away so much of me I used to be.

Stop It! Stop It! Before the hell on earth you created leads to a total damnation of your soul.

You, burning a little more each day in an eternal fire that never ends.

Stop It! Before you kill me, kill any chance of redemption.

Stop It! Before I rise up and take matters in my own hands.

Becoming just as sick and twisted as you by taking your life as a solution to end this strife and mutilation of my character.

Stop It! Stop It! Stop It! Can't you just pray and ask God to release the demons of relationship bullying?

Release you from being my tormenter instead of a protector and provider.

Stop It! For I am done!

I will no longer be the one wearing scars of your twisted mind.

Because, freely I loved you, and freely I go, gone, never to see you no more.

For finally, I've gained the strength to Stop It!

Dedicated to all those wounded people stuck in an abusive relationship.

Fury of a Woman's Scorn

Fury begins when I have reorganized my life, goals and objectives to better serve you, and you take all my sacrifices and multiple acts of kindness as something you have a God-given right to receive as we have a right to water and the air that we breathe.

Fury is nurtured when you continually are blindsided by your own illusion of greatness. As they say on the street, thoughts consume you of "I AM THE SHIT." Where you feel, anytime anyone experiences a part of you, they should be grateful.

Fury has reached epidemic proportions when your vices and flaws in the current reality are brought to your attention and you can't fathom what the hell I'm hallucinating about because, you are perfect!

When Fury has reached this level where communication has no longer become possible, it's time to know when to walk away and let others in their reality give them a wake-up call. As you move on to a relationship with more substance and more collaboration, give and take on both ends. Instead of giving your all to someone who only takes and retreats whenever he is asked to give.

Fury can have a better impression when it is unleashed in a mental mind game clothed in kindness and definitive strokes of retribution. When you walk away with dignity and let them know the best things in life can be free.

But a Payday will come, and their Pay-Up Day has arrived.

Ball, Book or Bike

Ball

There he goes with that fine chick that has supermodel status. Don't have to worry about how he pulled her 'cuz he be ballin'. Hanging out after school at elementary and middle schools and such. Polluting young minds with drugs to make him some gold dust. No thought process of the future generations he's helping destroy or corrupt. Because to him, it's just the easy way to make a buck.

Book

Here I am busting my ass every day working two jobs and neither pay more than minimum wage. Taking 18 hours in college this semester too. But that superfine woman don't want to hear about goals leading to my dreams being fulfilled.

She's only dealing with "right now money." My 4.0 grade point average and future CEO dreams are just that—a dream she sees as never happening. She can't conceptualize beyond her next Coach bag purchase. She has no clue all the white girls that see my potential but I don't step to because my heart and soul desires a black queen to share my dreams and the fruits of my labor.

Bike

Another day missing a gig due to transportation woes. Never any legit jobs in the hood. Always 10, 20 miles outside of the hood where you need a bike, car or bus to get there.

Why does the system encourage us to become criminals by forcing us to lie, steal and kill like animals to survive? Hey, I want to stay alive and live, not stay alive just to die a slow, painful existence on the street of my peoples.

Hey, what's your choice: BALL, BOOK or BIKE?

Young Blood

Kiss me. Hold me. Be with me.

For together, we can weather any storms, break out the norm,

Perform the impossible with the possible.

Kiss me, hold me, touch me, feel me up, baby,

Don't be shady, you suppose me to be a lady.

Baby, you need to revamp like Van Kamp and learn the stamp of approval is the removal of all doubt regarding where your loyalty lies.

My how time flies when you have arrived ahead of the game.

Ain't it a shame I can't call your name at the critical moment when the storm is raging.

So, baby, don't be staging or hazing; when I arise from these ashes and disguises, I arise as a MAN, no longer a victim of circumstances. A man with a plan in hand, seeking a woman that understands her place with her man. Not her arrival by happenstance or only when it will advance her cause.

Kiss me, hold me, touch me, baby. For together, we can weather any storms, break out the norm. But apart, you can only break my heart and start to show me what conceit and *just me* has done to the *we* that used to be and how that has disintegrated us.

Vandalicious

I know now that I loved you.

I know now that my problem was I had a fantasy vision of what I wanted from you that was not properly shared.

I know now we are two people with a shared physical passion for each other.

However, our life's passion is flowing in opposite directions.

I know now how much I needed the spontaneity and free, uninhibited reckless abandonment you brought into my life.

I needed the raw release you generated from the storms raging within me.

Thank you for being the first man ever to make me take responsibility for the fact that it did not work out.

A combination of miscommunicated dreams, unrealistic expectations and an unyielding impatience for wanting and needing to be in a relationship doomed us from the start.

I'll start praying now for patience and restraint so when the next Mr. Charming arrives, I can take it slow and get to know the real man and not the illusion of what I want him to be.

(Named "Vandalicious" because something that could have been so wonderful and unique was stolen, like a thief in the night, by impatience, unrealistic expectations and just bad timing all around.)

Brudda

There you are, tall, cocoa bronze, standing like a tree planted by the river, nurturing others through the warmth of your shade.

There you go representing a wonderful, secure, dependable asset in an ever-changing world.

There you are growing older, wiser and stronger in your convictions and your ability to finally articulate your plan of action for yourself.

There you are always allowing others close to you to determine your life plan by your perceived family commitment.

But here you are *now*, finally able to scrutinize your individual accomplishments and develop a plan based on what and how you want your future to be transformed.

There you go *finally* living your life like it's golden.

GOD BLESS YOU that you may continue to nourish the world with your unique version of personal comfort.

LOVE YOU MUCH.

Around Midnight

Around Midnight, the music encloses me and soothes the savage spaces of my existence.

Around Midnight, I can just be myself. No pretense or change of expression or worry about anyone else's existence, thought or feeling.

Around Midnight is my time to shine, decline or partake of the sublime.

Around Midnight is when I can get as freaky-deaky as I want to be, and all my inhibitions are released.

At the Crack of Dawn

At the Crack of Dawn, he had a heart on…fire from making love to me.

At the Crack of Dawn, we romanced and stayed entranced by the mystical depth of feeling our chemistry between us explored.

At the Crack of Dawn, my dreams came true as well as my fantasies.

At the Crack of Dawn, I was a pawn in his hands as he was a pawn in mine.

At the Crack of Dawn, our relationship moved on to the next level, never to be as we once were, just friends.

At the Crack of Dawn, our love solidified. We no longer could hide the Intensity of our Love.

For at this moment, we beat as one heart, one mind, one soul, which encompasses the whole of us.

At the Crack of Dawn, it was "ON, BABY."

Leroy's Kind of Love

Once in our lifetime, a woman needs a man who truly accepts her for all her pluses and minuses.

He was a man who was not intimidated by how much you brought to the table. Be that comrades of the opposite sex, girl friends, coworkers, business associates or exes from previous relationships.

A man who not only could stand up in it, but a woman's man.

He was confident, determined and sure of his love for you, and sure of what he brought to your relationship.

He basked in the glory of being with you and for you.

He, Leroy, enjoyed his ride-or-die girl, you… Mary.

He recognized your worth. Leroy saw you were his prize.

Now that GOD has taken him back to heaven to reunite him with all his ancestors gone before him, know, my girl, you extended his days and his happiness.

Whenever people saw you two together, no light bulb was needed. For the Love within your relationship glowed and poured out of both of you.

Take comfort in knowing Leroy, the man you loved, equally loved you in return.

Take comfort in knowing nothing was left unsaid between you.

Your getaway excursions to Mexico, Cuba and beyond are a testament to creative Lovemaking and sharing the best life you could have with each other.

I will pray for your strength as you transition from such a profound loss.

Leroy will forever be in your heart. He will forever cherish what you two had together.

It is now well with his soul. He has no more pain or physical limitations or suffering.

I love you, Mary, and want you to know I am proud to call you my Sistah–Girl.

Mr. Blu Collar Man

What's up, Mr. Blu Collar Man, who walks with pride, feeling all good inside, because every day you work from sun up to sunset feeling the sweat of your brow, toiling sometimes late into the night, using every muscle of your body to get the job done.

Even though your muscles ache, even though you worked through your lunch break, you smile because every ounce of your being speaks to a job well done at the end of the day.

Mr. Blu Collar Man, some people just don't understand the joy that comes from working every fiber of your being, mind, body and soul, to make a day's pay.

Mr. Blu Collar Man, your ecstasy is enhanced when you're working a job for a business that's all your own. It's like getting an orgasm every day.

Mr. Blu Collar Man, with your hands so rough and your walk of pride so tough, that only a smile of love could meet you at the end of the day.

A smile of thanks for putting your all into making the bacon, so I can buy the eggs, as we build a future together for yours and my dreams.

Mr. Blu Collar Man, you are just what the doctor ordered to smooth out my Professional Feathers and help calm down and unwind at the end of the day.

What's up, Mr. Blu Collar Man, with your hands so rough, hard and cracked you can feel the hammer in your groin with every stroke of your hand.

Mr. Blu Collar Man, every time your hands touch me, I feel the Intensity and Commitment that hewed those rough hands into getting the job done.

Mr. Blu Collar Man, you can be a part of my itinerary any day.

Mr. Huggstable

The joy and exuberance of being held close by a friend whose friendship has stood the test of time.

The tension and release of all physical barriers of distances and time since we last saw each other are erased as we cuddle and let go in each other's arms.

Damn, you felt good.

You Know How to Love Me

Today I reminisced about the gentleness of your lips brushing across my face in a spontaneous encounter. It reminded me why you are in my thoughts more than usual.

Your sincerity and ways of making the simplest of gestures feel intimate ignite a charge through my mental hot box.

This also fills my cheeks with a burst of joy, which is exhibited as a smile whenever I think of you. It is the small testaments of respect, honesty and trust that are the true building blocks of lasting intimacy.

Thank you once again for reminding me of the small touches that excite, ignite and help relationships remain fresh and endure the test of time.

Rain

Rain is symbolic of restless slumber. For when it rains, you want to sleep the day away. It is too ugly to want to be outside. The dreariness of rain tugs on our emotions and can cause a depressive anxiety to persist as we try to navigate happiness through a gloomy outlook.

Yet some days, rain can be a comfort, as the tiny wet droplets appear to cleanse the hurt, sorrow or agony we are feeling. There is no freedom like the freedom and reckless abandonment felt by walking in the rain without an umbrella and embracing a bad hair day head-on.

Rain is symbolic of restless slumber. For it is the perfect time to lie in bed and make love. You and yours have an easier time focusing on the two of you instead of the rest of us. For there truly is no other place you want to be.

Rain only stops Parades. Rain can be the beginning of a sensuous escapade as we try to create joy on a day when the atmosphere is stormy.

Rubber-Broke Babies

Joy of sex, pleasurable moments, moments when his arms are entangled in mine, and only the sensations heighten electricity that is created as an offshoot of the energy the two of us create.

There are no other beings in the universe as we work overtime absorbing each other's life fluids with frenzy.

We pound and pound into each other's being until we feel the cato-cosmic eruptions of our inner selves uniting and then collapsing in exhaustion as a joint climax is fulfilled.

Both of us know in our heart of hearts that this night was special.

Only later during cleanup do we notice that the rubber broke.

Then nine months later, we have a visual reminder of why that particular climax was so euphoric.

We created you, out of our selfish desires for a heightened sense of pleasure.

Not out of a desire to test boundaries of responsibility or commitment to a being that represents the best and worst of us. A being that will be a constant reminder that even the best-laid plans sometimes go astray.

So, today, I must say I love you, my rubber-broke baby.

Even though the intensity and excitement felt for your father has gone astray, my love for my rubber-broke baby surprise remains.

Wounded

Hey today, I take stock of my wounds. I realize how truly blessed I am that I'm still standing. Not bent, broke down or knocked down. Like the people I trounced or bounced off of on my way to do "My Thing." The thing that almost took me and them too. Hey, today, I know I am one of the lucky ones.

The invisible Wounded soldiers. Doing battle with an enemy you can't see. Doing battle with the innermost cravings and urges that war constantly within me for "Top Dog" attention. Attention! Now! Hey, though I sweat and smile, there are no visible tracks to be displayed. I am Wounded to the core. A victim of a bad score. Had to get my stomach pumped and much more before I faced the reality that if I didn't get help for me, I would pull everyone down around me. Hey, Wounded, that's me. But I got hope that someday I'll have the strength to cope without dope as the answer to my problems.

Time Shuttle

The windows of my mind are spinning like an out-of-control time machine trying to keep up with the fast pace of my existence. Looking for a respite adventure to slow down the pace of this rat race and free me some space to do me. You know, reacquaint me with me. So I can truly see what path I am on. And how my actions and mental window dressing actually expel energy and create the juices and vibrations for my future space and path.

The respite helps me consciously chart the future instead of allowing the task schedules others dictate to become my life force instead of consciously contributing to "My Life's Passion." Time Shuttle, trying to regulate the embryonic fluids of my existence and destiny.

Time Shuttle, a rebuttal to the workaholic definition of success in the Western societal mindset.

Time Shuttle, the tortoise crawl of relaxation and psychic exploration necessary to control my destiny.

There You Were

There you were in your elegant splendor.

There you were displaying your quiet poise.

There you were stating as one of few words.

You are beautiful; you intrigue me,

You, I would like to get to know better, if you don't mind.

There you were with your warm, subtle smile that hid the depth of your knowledge

And the warmth and compassion in your heart.

There you were offering just what I have waited a lifetime for.

There you were…

And suddenly, as time and space move on in an instant, the *there you were* became the *here you are*, and you were transported like in a vision or dream to me.

Thank you for displaying the essence of you, which is Sincerity, to the shell of me that desperately needed a change in script.

There you were, turned into the *there you are*, here, right now, with me, in my mind's eye, in my heart's open spaces and tonight on my lips in a prayer of thanksgiving for making me the recipient of such a priceless gift of you. The opportunity to spend one moment in time with you.

There you were, here you are, a memory of mine forever.

Dedicated to *Beaman, Beam me up Scottie,*
you make me Glow!

You and I

I am a unique black woman navigating in many worlds. I have numerous connections with my past. Varied responsibilities with the present, some mandatory, too many I volunteered for to actually complete. I have several visions, plans, dreams and commitments for the future.

YOU are a regimented, focused individual that lets very few, if anything, deter you from your flight plan. Your past molded you in character and purpose. Your present reality is to not get caught off guard by past mistakes. Your future is minimalistic: continuing education, being financially secure and continuing to operate in your passion.

Why our worlds have intersected at this time, in the universe, is still a mystery. Other than being Besties, I know not what the future holds for us.

However, I do know I must curb my impatience and spontaneity to allow our relationship to grow or fizzle at its own pace.

The Future Is Ours

Thinking of how our paths intersected with us meeting around live music, lifelong friends and poetry. As I reflect on our first encounter, it involved passion for our gifts, celebration of family. We spent the evening relaxing and allowing the music to calm our fears, stark realities, and just let go and let God for a few hours of respite for the week. Through this relationship, we have shared visions and supported each other's passions. We have uplifted and encouraged each other's children and families.

But the biggest gift we have experienced in our relationship has been honesty and genuine respect for each other.

Now that we are both experiencing empty nest and evaluating our futures, we find ourselves at a crossroads where we contemplate taking our friendship to a deeper commitment. It involves exploring a new depth of Intimacy in or relationship.

I promise to be vulnerable and open as we venture into these unchartered waters. I expect the same from you. I'm willing to carve out time and emotional support if you are willing to commit to weekly communication.

I am so looking forward to the future of us.

ABOUT THE AUTHOR

Spignotta Milam, a woman of many lifetimes and experiences.

Professionally, Spignotta has been a Licensed Clinical Social Worker for over 30 years. She has held numerous job titles such as assistant director of a homeless shelter; school social worker; individual, group, family and couple psychotherapist; substance abuse clinician; substitute teacher; storyteller and poet.

Spignotta has served on the board of a community center and is an active member of her sorority, Delta Sigma Theta. She also was a contributor of several scholarship initiatives with her sorority and Tennessee State University.

Spignotta is the mother of three phenomenally gifted adult children: two daughters and one son. She loves to travel, read, listen to live music and is actively involved with her church's children's ministry.

www.ingramcontent.com/pod-product-compliance
Ingram Content Group UK Ltd.
Pitfield, Milton Keynes, MK11 3LW, UK
UKHW041852190726
13854UKWH00002B/864

9 798987 293416